Till Death Do Us Part

D1565668

GILBERT COLEMAN, JR.

Published by

LIFEBRIDGE
B O O K S
P.O. BOX 49428
CHARLOTTE, NC 28277

Printed in the United States of America.

2

DEDICATION

*To my wife, Debi, who exemplifies
every principle found in this book—and makes
married life all it was meant to be.*

CONTENTS

CONTENTS
(CONTINUED)

1

Before You Say "I Do"

You are about to embark on the adventure of a lifetime—making a vow to spend the rest of your days with the person you love.

Are you truly prepared to enter into such a covenant? Do you really understand everything involved?

The reason you are engaged is not just to organize a wedding—this is simply an event which makes your union official. Instead, you are preparing for a *marriage* which embraces your entire future.

"MADE JUST FOR ME!"

When you look at history, the three great

institutions of the world are the church, the state and the home. Of these, the home is the oldest and most sacred since God Himself was involved in the union of Adam and Eve.

After He created man from the dust of the earth, God looked down and decided, *"It is not good that man should be alone; I will make him a helper..."* (Genesis 2:18).

I've heard young men excitedly exclaim about their bride, "She was made just for me!" Well, the first man could have said the same thing because the Creator took one of Adam's ribs and formed a mate for him. Adam said, *"This is now bone of my bones and flesh of my flesh: She shall be called Woman, because she was taken out of Man"* (v.23).

OUR BEDROCK

Scripture gives us this instruction: *"Therefore a man shall leave his father and mother and be joined to his wife, and they shall become one flesh"* (v.24).

What was the Almighty looking for in this union? *"He seeks godly offspring"* (Malachi 2:15).

As a believer, you need to understand that it is God

Himself who initiates and establishes marriage so there will be *sacred* homes, lead by *sacred* couples, producing *sacred* children. This is central to the plan of His Kingdom.

For this reason—because of procreation—in God's sight a marriage is to take place between one man and one woman. There is absolutely no alternative arrangement.

Without the home and family as the foundation, there can be no order, society, government or even the church.

It is the bedrock of our stability and security here on earth.

A SPIRITUAL UNION

The marital adventure which you are just beginning is more than sharing time and emotions with a partner; you are building a life together. This means sacrifice, time, work, energy, effort and responsibility. Instead of two individuals with separate goals and objectives, they are merged into one purpose and destiny.

Most important, however, is that you are united spiritually before you become joined physically. As a minister, I have seen the tragic results of marriages where one partner "talks the talk" of a Christian just to obtain the "prize," yet there is no real commitment of the heart.

"LIGHT AND DARKNESS"

Take whatever time you need to make absolutely certain the person with whom you will exchange vows truly knows the Lord. I'm not talking of an individual who attends church with you because he or she thinks it makes you happy. The answer must be an unequivocal "Yes" to these questions:

- Does she have a personal testimony of the saving grace of Christ?
- Does he read God's Word daily?
- Is there a hunger for the things of the Lord?
- Are you on the same page "theologically?"

The Bible gives us this warning: *"Do not be unequally yoked together with unbelievers. For what fellowship has righteousness with lawlessness? And what communion has light with darkness?"* (2 Corinthians 6:14).

We must not be seduced by our emotions, believing somehow, someday our partner will come to accept Christ.

Even if it means the embarrassment of delaying your marriage or breaking off the relationship, make certain the person you cherish also loves God.

ADDRESS THE ISSUES NOW

Since true love is a priceless gift from above, it is totally impossible for us to understand the depth of its meaning without a divine relationship with our Heavenly Father.

Agape love, or the "God kind of love" transcends anything we can experience on our own. This is why it is imperative for the Holy Spirit to be active in both of your lives.

God is asking you to resemble His character, His Word and His principles. If this is not evident before you repeat the vows of marriage, how can you expect it to be present later?

For example, if you have regular arguments and daily shouting matches over minor issues, I can guarantee the decibel levels and physical skirmishes will only escalate on the other side of the altar. This is why I urge you to address the matters now—and take the issues before the Lord until there is peace and harmony in the relationship.

I'm not implying that once you are husband and wife you will never have disagreements, but if you learn how to prayerfully resolve your differences today, you'll know what to do when trouble rears its ugly head tomorrow.

YOUR PLEDGE

Spiritual maturity starts *before* marriage. If losing your temper is a continual problem for either of you, stop yelling and start quietly communicating. Remember, *"The heart is deceitful above all things, and desperately wicked"* (Jeremiah 17:9). This is why we must personally put God's principles into practice. *"Let all bitterness, wrath, anger, clamor, and evil speaking be put away from you, with all malice. And be kind to one another, tenderhearted, forgiving one another, even as God in Christ forgave you"* (Ephesians 4:31-32).

Decide *today* how you will conduct yourself before God and your mate. For instance, make a pledge to the Lord you will never speak critically of the one you love behind his or her back—not even to your own family. Why? Because according to Scripture, *"...every idle word men may speak, they will give account of it in the day of judgment"* (Matthew 12:36).

Let me encourage you to be open and honest with the Holy Spirit so God can remove any habits, attitudes or negative tendencies and allow you to be a godly example in your marriage.

WHOSE OPINION?

Your relationship must, above all, glorify God. This is demonstrated in the "little" things you do for your future spouse—including recognizing the other person's feelings and not always trying to be dominant and constantly in control. Discard the "My way or the highway" mentality.

Ask the Lord to "temper" your sensitivity and gift you with the ability to rise above the hurts of life.

Recognize the fact there are three opinions in every relationship: his, her's and God's. In the final analysis there is only one opinion which counts—and you know whose it is!

Ask yourself, "What does the *Lord* say concerning the situation?" "What does the *Word* declare on the matter?" As a couple, allow the Holy Spirit to, *"...guide you into all truth"* (John 16:13).

Serious Implications

Your upcoming wedding is not just an extravagant party with designer clothes, limousines and a honeymoon in the sun. This is all "surface" and show!

When you become serious enough with another human being to contemplate announcing your engagement and eventual marriage, take a deep, insightful, serious look at all this commitment implies.

If you have been a guest at a wedding, perhaps you have heard a minister utter these words: "Marriage is not to be entered into unadvisedly or lightly, but reverently, discreetly, soberly and in the fear of God."

The word "unadvisedly" is significant. It means you should seek godly direction before matrimony. What you will learn from this book is essential, but let me encourage you to also spend time with a pastor or Christian counselor. Have an open heart to the guidance you receive.

An Honorable Journey

As we will learn, marriage is holy and the Father's righteousness is to be seen in the relationship and His truth perpetuated. It is *"...honorable among all, and the bed undefiled"* (Hebrews 13:4).

Your search for a spouse should not be based on the fact you are tired of being alone. Love and marriage is a noble, honorable, and reverential journey.

The vows you are about to take—which we will examine line by line—are not only made to your spouse, but pledged to Almighty God Himself. As you will discover, only He can make the adventure complete.

2

"We are gathered here in the sight of God and in the presence of these witnesses..."

The big day has finally arrived. Every detail has been double-checked—gowns, tuxedos, flowers, limos, photographers and musicians.

Ushers have seated the invited guests, the groomsmen are standing at attention, and while the organ plays Wagner's beloved "Here Comes the Bride," all eyes turn to watch the soon-to-be-married beauty being escorted down the center aisle of the chapel.

When the bridal party is in place, the minister stands before the bride and groom and announces, "We are gathered here today in the sight of God and in the presence of these witnesses to join together this man and this woman in holy matrimony."

YEARS OF DREAMING

In the vast majority of cases, the radiant bride who is standing at the front of the church is far more prepared for this moment than the man.

The training started early when she began playing with her "Ken and Barbie" dolls—and creating make-believe relationships. She spent countless hours with her little girl friends enjoying pretend "tea parties" and feeding a bottle to her plastic "baby."

Where was the future groom? He was rough and tumbling out in the backyard with his cowboy hat and pistol—or perhaps mimicking G.I. Joe, mowing down the enemy with a toy bazooka!

So long before her real wedding, the bride was flipping through magazines, planning the colors of her attendant's dresses and envisioning what this special day would be like. For years she has dreamed of finding, "Mr. Right," decorating her own home and starting a family. Such detailed preparation gives her tremendous confidence and optimism.

The groom, however, likely never took the time to contemplate such things. All he knows is the here and now; standing at the altar with the love of his life. His heart is pumping overtime—and he is petrified!

THE "THIRD PARTY"

The words spoken by the minister, "in the sight of God" are not randomly chosen. Of all those who are present for the ceremony, Almighty God is the "Chief Witness." After all, it is the Creator who initiated the entire process—bringing the first man and woman together in the Garden of Eden.

As bride and groom it is only natural to be caught up in the emotion of the moment.

Perhaps you find it difficult to take your eyes off each other, yet you need to realize there is a third party involved in the union. God is at the center of what is taking place.

Since weddings have become a $40 billion dollar

annual industry in America, we can easily become so distracted by the "trappings" of the event that the real meaning and purpose of the ceremony often takes a back seat.

A PATTERN TO FOLLOW

We must never allow the excitement of the day to blur the fact that marriage is an institution of God and has its basis in the divine revelation of Holy Scriptures. From the time the Lord decreed, "...a *man shall leave his father and mother and be joined to his wife*" (Genesis 2:24), it was obvious that the union of a man and woman was both physical and spiritual.

The Maker introduced this amazing "experience of love" so we could establish a social order on earth and build a pattern for well-ordered families whose values would be passed down from one generation to the next.

Jesus Himself honored a marriage celebration in Cana with His presence (John 2). It is also significant that He chose this occasion to perform His first miracle—turning water into wine.

Later, the Holy Spirit, speaking through the apostle Paul, used the symbol of a husband and wife to represent the union which binds together Christ and His own blood-bought, ransomed church. *"Husbands, love your wives, just as Christ also loved the church and gave Himself for her"* (Ephesians 5:25).

"AS A BRIDE"

The unique and vital relationship between God and marriage is woven throughout Scripture:

- *"And as the bridegroom rejoices over the bride, so shall your God rejoice over you"* (Isaiah 62:5).
- The Lords says, *"Return, O backsliding children...for I am married to you...and I will bring you to Zion"* (Jeremiah 3:14).
- John saw, *"...the holy city, New Jerusalem, coming down out of heaven from God,*

21

prepared as a bride adorned for her husband" (Revelation 21:2).

THE "WITNESSES"

The friends and loved ones who attend your wedding ceremony are far more than invited guests; they are actual witnesses who have come to observe the fact you are taking a lifetime vow of marriage before God. This is why the minister includes the words, "in the face of this company," or "in the presence of these witnesses."

From this moment on, these people will attest that you have made a commitment to each other which you intend to keep.

If you have invited 200 guests to your wedding, there are now 200 individuals to whom you will forever be answerable. This is no small commitment.

WHAT DOES THE LORD EXPECT?

Sadly, many couples enter into matrimony without giving one thought to the ordinances and vows included in the ceremony. Their mindset is, "Let's get this over with. What the minister says is just

TILL DEATH DO US PART

tradition—and we are supposed to reply 'I will' and 'I do' to all his questions."

Even believers who have been raised in the church often have a nonchalant, "Who cares?" attitude toward the pledge they are being asked to repeat. They treat the vows as a formality.

Just because those who live by the world's standards may regard their commitments lightly does not give you free licence to stray from God's ordinances.

Instead of following the pack, accepting the behavior of culture and society, prayerfully ask yourself, "What does the Lord expect of me? How does He view the commitment I am about to make?"

YOUR DIVINE COMMITMENT

A godly marriage is to be an example for others to follow. As children of God, we *set* the standards—not follow them. This is why Scripture declares, *"Come out from among them and be separate, says the Lord"* (2 Corinthians 6:17).

Because others may treat their vows as flippant phrases which can later be retracted doesn't give us the same option.

As you stand before the altar of matrimony, you have been given the opportunity to let your light so shine that it will *"...glorify your Father in heaven"* (Matthew 5:16).

Pause for a moment and contemplate the moral principles you are being commanded to keep.

Every word you say has eternal consequences.

3

"...to join this man and this woman in holy matrimony."

$\mathcal{G}$od decrees that in marriage, two shall be as one. When you consider the diverse uniqueness of individuals, this in itself is a miracle.

- How can a man who is used to throwing his dirty laundry on the floor live with a woman who is a perfectionist?
- How does a woman who loses her temper at the least provocation co-exist with a mild-mannered mate?
- What if she is a night-owl and he is an early riser?

■ What if he only wants to watch the news
and she loves movies?

Let's face it, there is far more than a physical
difference between men and women. In a recent
Gallup poll, women were seen as emotional, talkative,
patient, creative and affectionate, while men were
viewed as more aggressive, courageous and ambitious.

Yes, the joining of two distinct, separate
personalities can be a jolt to the system, but since this
is God's eternal plan, He gives us the ability to make
the necessary adjustments.

FROM DUST!

To better understand the roles of male and female,
consider how we were made.

Man is "refined dust" because God formed him
from the dust of the earth—then breathed His own
divine breath into him.

One of the reasons God is so longsuffering, merciful
and forgiving is because He understands who we are
and how we were created. Scripture declares, *"As a
father has compassion on his children, so the Lord has*

compassion on those who fear him; for he knows how we are formed, he remembers that we are dust" (Psalm 103:13-14 NIV).

The woman, however, is *doubly refined* dust since she came from the rib of Adam rather than the earth itself. Later, we will discuss the significance of Eve being taken from Adam's side.

Since sand and dust can be blown away, it is only natural that a great deal of settling and shaping needs to occur in us. For example, every couple can recount the "stupid" things they did while they were young or dating, but this is no excuse to continue the pattern after marriage.

After bringing you together, you'll be tested by the Lord again and again to see if you are growing and maturing into the persons He expects you to be.

THE CROWN!

God's Word establishes man as the head of the

household (Ephesians 5:23), while the woman is the "crown" which rests on his head. The Bible says, *"An excellent wife is the crown of her husband"* (Proverbs 12:4).

She is the *glory* of the man—and as such holds a place of high esteem in the union. She is also honored in Scripture for her beauty, value and character (Proverbs 31). As a result, *"Her children rise up and call her blessed; her husband also, and he praises her"* (v.28).

THE "ADAM" ELEMENT

Wouldn't it be wonderful if the marriage ceremony was so life-transforming that any problems you brought with you would suddenly disappear into thin air? Let me assure you, this is fantasy.

You see, each individual must personally deal with the fact he or she was born in sin and only through repentance can a heart and life be changed.

The Bible tells us, *"...through one man* [Adam] *sin entered the world, and death through sin, and thus death spread to all men, because all sinned"* (Romans 5:12). Then comes the good news: *"But where sin abounded, grace abounded much more, so that as sin reigned in death, even so grace might reign through righteousness to eternal life through Jesus Christ our Lord"* (vv.20-21).

THE WARNING

The chasm between God and man—and even between man and woman—can be traced to the Tree of the Knowledge of Good and Evil in the Garden of Eden. Unfortunately, some still have the root of that Tree residing inside of them.

Adam was placed in charge of this earthly paradise and was told only one item was off-limits. God said, *"Of every tree of the garden you may freely eat; but of the tree of the knowledge of good and evil you shall not eat, for in the day that you eat of it you shall surely die"* (Genesis:2:16-17).

It was immediately after issuing this warning, God

29

brought Adam a wife. Before this time he was surrounded by animals—then suddenly he was presented with the most wonderful creature he had ever seen: a woman. He was smitten by her awesome beauty.

AN EVIL ENTICEMENT

When Eve entered the scene, Adam shared this command of the Creator with her, yet Satan, disguised in the form of a serpent, slithered up to the woman and whispered, *"You will not surely die. For God knows that in the day you eat of it your eyes will be opened, and you will be like God, knowing good and evil"* (Genesis 3:4).

As the sly serpent approached Eve, he didn't entice her with what might cause her harm. He lied and offered enlightenment—even divine knowledge.

Tragically, Eve listened to Satan. She *"...saw that the tree was good for food, that it was pleasant to the eyes, and a tree desirable to make one wise, she took of its fruit and ate. She also gave to her husband with her, and he ate"* (v.6).

At that moment their innocence disappeared. As a

result, they saw their nakedness and tried to cover their bodies.

SHIFTING THE BLAME!

Next, while walking in the Garden, God spoke, asking, "Where are you?"

Adam replied, *"I heard Your voice...and I was afraid because I was naked; and I hid myself"* (v.10)

The Creator questioned, *"Who told you that you were naked? Have you eaten from the tree of which I commanded you that you should not eat?"* (v.11).

Then came Adam's excuse: *"The woman whom You gave to be with me, she gave me of the tree, and I ate"* (v.12).

Talk about shifting the blame! First, he faulted God for the woman "You gave me," then he blamed his wife, saying, "she gave me of the tree."

REMOVE THE ROOT!

It is sad to observe how when problems arise in a

marriage, we don't listen to what the Lord has to say. Adam knew God's command, but was so taken with his earthy companion he blindly followed her ill-informed advice.

Let's face it. When you meet "Mr. Right" or "Miss America," your hormones start raging to the point you would follow your new love right off the edge of a cliff!

Stop for a moment and ask yourself, "Is a stubborn root from the Tree still residing in me? Has the sin in my life been removed and covered by the blood of the Savior?"

Ask the Holy Spirit to extract every small particle of iniquity from your heart and start living by faith instead of being led by the flesh.

HEART-TO-HEART

If you have never asked Christ to forgive your sin and become the Lord of your life, do not delay another day to make this commitment. The same must be true for the person you are about to marry.

Don't be embarrassed or hesitant to have a heart-to-heart talk with your future spouse regarding repentance, salvation and what it means to be "born again." In fact, I highly recommend you open God's Word and study together what Scripture declares on the matter:

- *"Except a man be born again, he cannot see the kingdom of God"* (John 3:3 KJV).
- *"For God so loved the world that He gave His only begotten Son, that whoever believes in Him should not perish but have everlasting life"* (John 3:16).
- *"But as many as received Him, to them He gave the right to become children of God, to those who believe in His name"* (John 1:12).
- *"Therefore, if anyone is in Christ, he is a new creation; old things have passed away; behold, all things have become new"* (2 Corinthians 5:17).

Let me also encourage you to read these additional verses: Romans 5:15; 2 Corinthians 5:21; Ephesians 2:1; Colossians 2:13; 1 Timothy 2:3-4: 4:9-10; Titus 3:4-6; 1 John 2:1-2. They will give you a greater understanding of salvation.

You can receive Christ's forgiveness anywhere, at any time.

I can't begin to explain how imperative it is for you to enter "holy matrimony" knowing your sins have been erased and you are washed in the precious blood Christ shed for you at Calvary.

A SURE FOUNDATION

Please take one more step of faith. Before your marriage, during a church service when an invitation is given for you to publicly accept Christ as your personal Savior, both of you should walk to the altar and make this declaration—even if one of you has previously accepted the Lord.

Making a stand before God and man seals it in your heart and confirms to the world that you are serious about beginning a new life together with Christ.

Marriage is the second most important step you will ever take. The first is your soul's salvation. When the foundation is secure, what is established by God will transform the dust of your life into solid ground.

Allow the Almighty to put the "holy" in holy matrimony.

4

"Speak now, or forever hold your peace."

*C*enturies ago, when arranged marriages were much more common than today, the father of the bride was required to provide a dowry.

During the ceremony, the question was asked, "If any person can show just cause why this couple may not lawfully be joined together, let them now speak or forever hold their peace."

If the father had not fulfilled his part of the bargain, this was the last chance for the groom's family to complain. After this, it would be too late.

Today, these words still remain part of most wedding ceremonies—for good reason. The bride and groom need to take an honest, sober look at their past and make certain yesterday has been properly dealt with. Standing before the altar of marriage is no time to be living a lie.

A BIG MISTAKE?

As a minister, every time I reach this part of the ceremony, I wonder, "Would anyone dare speak up at a moment like this?"

Yet, seated in the audience there may be some guest who has thought, "She is making a big mistake," or "He should not be marrying this person."

Perhaps you have seen them bicker and argue the entire time they have been dating, or you believe there is no real bond of love between them—nothing to cement them together.

Now you are attending their wedding with your eyes lowered, silently saying, "Lord, this should not be happening!"

Because you don't want to be the bearer of truth or draw attention to yourself, you keep quiet—worried more about saving face than preventing an unhappy marriage. But when the reception is over and the confetti has been tossed, you can't wait to get on the phone and become the prophet of doom over the future of the newlyweds.

I certainly don't encourage interrupting a wedding since there is a much more civilized way to handle the matter. If you have any just reason (other than your personal opinion) why an engaged couple should not enter into matrimony, you have an obligation to meet with either or both to state your case. The actual wedding day certainly isn't the time.

This part of the ceremony was initially instituted to give the father of the bride the opportunity to call off the wedding if the father of the groom had not paid all of the agreed-upon dowry. Today, it is an opportunity to begin the marriage on a foundation of truth.

"CONFESS IT NOW"

To me, the most important part of the "charge" is not to outsiders who may have an objection, rather to the couple themselves. Before taking their vows, they need to contemplate these words:

"I require and charge you both, as you will answer in the dreadful day of judgment when the secrets of all hearts shall be disclosed, that if either one of you know why you should not be together, why you cannot be lawfully joined together in matrimony, confess it now. For be assured that if any persons are joined together other than God's Word allows, your marriage is unlawful."

PRE-MARITAL SEX

The laws of society will tolerate many things God's Word does not allow. This is why we need to examine our actions carefully in light of Scripture.

For example, the Almighty does not condone sex of any kind outside of marriage. However, you may ask, "What if the person I am marrying was living with someone else before we met? Does this mean we cannot marry?"

Thankfully, I am not God, yet I know how seriously He regards the matter. Fornication—pre-marital sex—is against God's law. Paul writes, *"Do not be deceived. Neither fornicators, nor idolaters, nor adulterers, nor homosexuals, nor sodomites, nor thieves, nor covetous, nor drunkards, nor revilers, nor extortioners will inherit the kingdom of God"* (1 Corinthians 6:9-10).

"WASHED" AND "JUSTIFIED"

You may complain, "That's rather harsh!

If you continue reading the next verse you'll find the solution. The apostle Paul says, *"And such were some of you"* (v.11). He is speaking to the believers at Corinth who had obviously committed one or more of these transgression in the past. Then he states, *"But you were washed, but you were sanctified, but you were justified in the name of the Lord Jesus and by the Spirit of our God"* (v.11).

I believe our Heavenly Father treats a person who knowingly sins much more harshly than one who does not know the Word.

In either case, however, the Father's door of repentance and forgiveness is always open.

The Bible gives us this counsel: *"Flee sexual immorality. Every sin that a man does is outside the body, but he who commits sexual immorality sins against his own body. Or do you not know that your body is the temple of the Holy Spirit who is in you, whom you have from God, and you are not your own? For you were bought at a price; therefore glorify God in your body and in your spirit, which are God's"* (vv.18-20).

LET GOD BURY THE PAST

To "repent" means to turn around and start walking in a new direction. You own up and confess to what was wrong, ask His forgiveness and promise the Lord, "I will never do that again."

As you approach your wedding day, make certain your past has been buried in the sea of God's forgetfulness. He promises, *"...their sin I will remember no more"* (Jeremiah 31:34).

"WHO GIVES THIS WOMAN?"

It is essential for both parties to be prepared for every aspect of marriage—especially the husband-to-be. A tremendous duty and obligation is now being placed on his shoulders.

At a designated point in the ceremony, the minister will say, "Who gives this woman to be married to this man?" It is usually the father, who proudly replies, "I do!"

This signifies a transfer of responsibility. The parents have been held accountable for the young woman up to this point. But remember, God is also the Father of the bride and He is counting on this groom to take care of His daughter the same way He has looked after her.

PROTECTOR AND PARTNER

Let me address these remarks to the groom. Woman was not taken from Adam's foot so you could step on her; nor was she formed from his head so you could dominate her. She was taken from a rib—under Adam's arm—so you could protect her.

You are not called to be her lord and master. She was taken from man's side because she is your equal—and she came from a place close to the heart so you could love her.

Yes, you are her "protector," and also her partner.

The woman standing beside you is not just a beautiful shell with no goals and desires of her own. She is your soulmate who needs your love and protection for the adventure ahead.

Are you prepared to accept this responsibility?

5

"You are entering into a sacred, eternal covenant ordained by God."

*O*ver five million couples in America are living together out of wedlock. Some, after "shacking up" for months or years, finally say, "Let's get married so we can make it legal." However, there is a great difference between an earthly contract based on the laws of the state and a covenant before God which is founded on faith, trust and commitment.

The union between a man and woman established by the Creator was never meant to be a "trial marriage," yet some treat the process like test-driving a car before making their purchase!

"JUST THE WAY YOU ARE"

Instead of a making a casual commitment, as part of the ceremony you will hear these words: "You are entering into a sacred, eternal covenant ordained by God."

The officiating minister asks the groom this thought-provoking question: "Will you, _____, take this woman to be your wedded wife, to live together after God's ordinance in the holy estate of matrimony?" And later he will address the bride, "Will you, _____, take this man to be your wedded husband..."

———— ☺ ————

The word "take" means "to accept or to agree." You're publicly admitting, "I accept you just the way you are."

You also agree, "to have and to hold, from this day forward." In addition to the physical aspect "to have," you also promise to "hold" your spouse in your mind and think of none other for the rest of your days.

The foundation for your relationship is based on

God's ordinance—not what you have gleaned from Oprah or Dr. Phil! And the vows you exchange are holy—and permanent.

GOD DESPISES DIVORCE!

It is discouraging to read the statistics that approximately half of all marriages will end in divorce—and the rate is shockingly similar for Christians and non-Christians alike.

The Bible has much to say on this subject, but the bottom line is: God despises divorce! The Word teaches, *"...let none deal treacherously with the wife of his youth. For the Lord God of Israel says that He hates divorce, for it covers one's garment with violence"* (Malachi 3:15-16).

Among ministers of the Gospel, the general consensus is there are only two valid reasons for divorce: (1) physical abuse and (2) adultery.

No spouse is to "defile" the other. The Bible states, *"Do you not know that you are the temple of God and that the Spirit of God dwells in you? If anyone defiles the temple of God, God will destroy him. For the temple of God is holy, which temple you are"* (1 Corinthians 3:16-17).

Physical, mental or emotional abuse
of any kind is abhorrent to God.

THE ISSUE OF ADULTERY

Regarding adultery, Jesus addressed the subject head on. In Judea, the Pharisees tested Him, asking, *"Is it lawful for a man to divorce his wife for just any reason?"* (Matthew 19:3).

Jesus answered the critics, saying, *"Have you not read that He who made them at the beginning 'made them male and female,' and said, 'For this reason a man shall leave his father and mother and be joined to his wife, and the two shall become one flesh'? So then, they are no longer two but one flesh. Therefore what God has joined together, let not man separate"* (vv.4-6).

They questioned Jesus even further: *"Why then did Moses command to give a certificate of divorce, and to put her away?"* (v.7).

Here was the Lord's answer to the Pharisees,

"Moses, because of the hardness of your hearts, permitted you to divorce your wives, but from the beginning it was not so. And I say to you, whoever divorces his wife, except for sexual immorality, and marries another, commits adultery; and whoever marries her who is divorced commits adultery" (vv.8-9).

This was the same message Jesus gave in His "Sermon on the Mount." He taught *"Furthermore it has been said, 'Whoever divorces his wife, let him give her a certificate of divorce.' But I say to you that whoever divorces his wife for any reason except sexual immorality causes her to commit adultery; and whoever marries a woman who is divorced commits adultery"* (Matthew 5:31:33).

NO FLIMSY EXCUSES

There have been cases when, after tying the knot, one of the parties discovers the spouse has been previously married and never divorced. The individual was living in adultery and didn't even know it! This is why I recommend that if there is the slightest doubt, have a professional conduct a federal background check.

Yes, there may be rare instances where divorce is justified, but the vows of marriage are to be an "eternal covenant"—not a bond to be broken for selfish reasons or flimsy excuses such as "incompatibility."

Paul taught *"...the woman who has a husband is bound by the law to her as long as she lives"* (Romans 7:2). Then he added, *"But if the husband dies, she is released from the law of her husband. So then if, while her husband lives, she marries another man, she will be called an adulteress; but if her husband dies, she is free from that law, so that she is no adulteress, though she has married another man"* (vv. 2-3).

The ultimate marriage, however, is to Christ. This is why Paul said we should *"...be married to another—to Him who was raised from the dead, that we should bear fruit to God"* (v.4).

"I AM NOT LEAVING"

Together, make the decision that the word "divorce" will not be tolerated in your household. Both of you should arrive at the same conclusion: "Come hell or high water, I am not leaving this marriage."

*If God has joined you together,
how can you have the audacity to
tear the union apart? In the name of
Jesus, bind the spirit of division.*

Since the Bible declares, *"Love never fails"* (1 Corinthians 13:8), what gives you the right to say "I'm not in love anymore"? Remember, God is love; thus, to say you are no longer in love implies that God has failed!

Most couples who divorce usually give minimum thought to those who are going to be affected by their actions—especially the children.

They are banking on the resiliency of the kids to bounce back and make the adjustment. Instead they may be facing bitter custody battles, pitting one parent against the other—while the children continue to suffer.

WHAT ABOUT TOMORROW?

"I just can't take it anymore," is not an excuse. You

51

don't have a biblical leg to stand on! Nowhere in Scripture can you find justification for using such logic to break up the home.

As parents, we must make certain we do not create further generations of shattered families.

The psalmist tells us how God, *"...established a testimony in Jacob, and appointed a law in Israel, which He commanded our fathers, that they should make them known to their children; That the generation to come might know them, the children who would be born, that they may arise and declare them to their children, That they may set their hope in God, and not forget the works of God, but keep His commandments; and may not be like their fathers, a stubborn and rebellious generation, a generation that did not set its heart aright, and whose spirit was not faithful to God"* (Psalm 78:5-8).

I pray we will be faithful to our vows so our children will not repeat our self-centered mistakes.

AN ETERNAL COMMITMENT

The statistics of divorce are bad enough, yet millions more are essentially separated in their own homes—sleeping in separate beds, not communicating with one another, and living through a marriage nightmare.

Why does this happen? Because we choose to expose the flaws of our spouse instead of covering them. We are not sensitive to his or her needs and we fail to make God's Word the cornerstone of our actions and behavior.

The vows you take at marriage are a sacred and *eternal* covenant. God has performed His part; will you be faithful to yours?

6

"Will you love and comfort...?"

*F*or decades, society has clashed over the fact the wording of the wedding vows for the groom differ from that of the bride.

During the ceremony, the man is questioned, "Will you love her, comfort her, honor her...?" While the woman is asked, "Will you obey him and serve him, love, honor and keep him...."?

Some brides insist the words "obey" and "serve" should be deleted from the ceremony, but let me share with you why I believe they are still an essential ingredient of the vows. It is a spiritual, biblical matter—and God's plan for placing structure and order in the home.

The apostle Paul taught the early believers, *"Wives, submit to your own husbands, as to the Lord. For the husband is head of the wife, as also Christ is head of the church; and He is the Savior of the body. Therefore, just as the church is subject to Christ, so let the wives be to their own husbands in everything"* (Ephesians 5:22-23).

A SPIRITUAL PARALLEL

Please know that despite popular opinion, "obey" and "serve" cannot be removed from God's Word. Wives are to be *"...obedient to their own husbands, that the word of God may not be blasphemed"* (Titus 2:5).

Some may question, "How can I possibly submit to a man whose behavior and attitude isn't what I expected?"

According to Scripture, a woman's obedience in marriage should parallel and demonstrate her submission to the Lord.

A Christian marriage is supposed to reflect the relationship between Christ and the church; this is what Paul was actually speaking of in Ephesians 5. We focus more on the negatives instead of seeing what he was referring to. Paul writes, *"This is a great mystery, but I speak concerning Christ and the church"* (Ephesians 5:32).

You should respond to your husband's request as long as it does not cause you to compromise the Word of God. His role is not to become your lord and master, rather a benevolent servant leader.

With the exception of physical abuse or adultery, the wife is to love and obey her spouse. Sadly, some women acquiesce to their boss at work far more than they serve their husband at home.

YOUR INFLUENCE

To better understand the spiritual significance and impact the behavior a wife has on her husband, Peter writes, *"For you were like sheep going astray, but have now returned to the Shepherd and Overseer of your souls" (1 Peter 2:25).*

Then we read, *"Wives, likewise, be submissive to your own husbands, that even if some do not obey the word, they, without a word, may be won by the conduct of their wives, when they observe your chaste conduct"* (1 Peter 3:1-2).

HIDDEN BEAUTY

If you are a born again Christian, yet your husband wants nothing to do with church, don't continually nag him regarding his spiritual health or "beat him over the head with the Bible."

Centuries ago, King Solomon wisely wrote, it is *"Better to dwell in a corner of a housetop, than in a house shared with a contentious woman"* (Proverbs 21:9).

Today if you are praying for the man you love to change his behavior, try demonstrating God's principles through your daily conduct.

Scripture also offers this important counsel: *"Do*

not let your adornment be merely outward—arranging the hair, wearing gold, or putting on fine apparel —rather let it be the hidden person of the heart, with the incorruptible beauty of a gentle and quiet spirit, which is very precious in the sight of God" (1 Peter 3:3-4).

This is how your husband will see your true beauty.

Does this mean you must allow a man to belittle you? No.

Raging through the house, slamming doors and rolling your eyes in disgust is not God's plan for you. Marriage is a test of your relationship with God. In fact, every biblical principle you have ever learned, or will learn, will be tested in marriage.

Remember, a spirit of gentleness is treasured in the eyes of your Heavenly Father.

UNCONDITIONAL LOVE

As you stand before the wedding altar you are publicly declaring, "This man has the ability to lead me and I have no problem placing the remainder of my life in his hands."

You are to love him unconditionally
—even though he gains a few pounds,
develops a receding hairline or
snores like a bear at night!

A WORD TO THE GROOM

Men, you're not off the hook!

The Bible offers clear guidance regarding how you are to treat your wife—and it's never with a domineering, authoritative attitude.

Just after Paul instructs a woman to be submissive to her spouse, he says, *"So husbands ought to love their own wives as their own bodies; he who loves his wife loves himself. For no one ever hated his own flesh, but nourishes and cherishes it, just as the Lord does the church"* (Ephesians 5:28-29)

Peter gives this admonition: *"Husbands, likewise, dwell with them with understanding, giving honor to the wife, as to the weaker vessel, and as being heirs together of the grace of life, that your prayers may not be hindered"* (1 Peter 3:7).

Don't misunderstand what Paul says—a woman is not weak by any stretch of the imagination.

"Praise Her!"

As a husband you are to "love and cherish" your wife. She is a treasured gift being presented to you.

The moment you unwrap this gift, she is yours—and you can't send her back for a replacement.

The word "cherish" means "to keep warm." Let her know she is protected and you will always be there for her; sensitive to her needs at those times when she needs to talk.

If she changes her hair style, compliment her. As the Bible says, *"Her husband...praises her"* (Proverbs 31:28).

When she prepares your favorite meal, thank her for standing over a hot stove—never take her for granted in any aspect of your relationship. Remember, she is not simply a sex object.

"DON'T WORRY"

During the ceremony, the groom is asked, "Wilt thou comfort her?"

If you don't already know, you will soon learn a woman doesn't deal with issues in the same manner you do. This means when she is emotionally fragile, be understanding of her needs. At such times, place your arms around her and comfort her with loving words, assuring her, "I'm right here. Don't worry about a thing."

Likewise, when the husband is passing through a period of trial and testing, the wife is to be his solace. When he turns to you, he should be able to find the rest and peace he is looking for—and I am not just referring to sexual intimacy.

Your feminine radar should be able
to pick up when there's something
negative occurring in his life.

Hug him and let him know, "I love you. Together, we're going to make it through this."

Your smile should be as warm as the sun and your voice as sweet music to gently calm his fears. As Solomon writes, *"...the heart of her husband safely trusts her; so he will have no lack of gain. She does him good and not evil all the days of her life"* (Proverbs 31:11-12).

THE FINAL WORD

Marriages work best when both the husband and wife are constantly communicating and continually *"...submitting to one another in the fear of God"* (Ephesians 5:21). Yet, during those rare times when the two of you cannot reach an agreement, according to the principles of Scripture, the final word belongs to the man.

If a woman feels she cannot handle this arrangement, perhaps it is better she never marries.

HOPES AND DREAMS

To keep the spark of love alive and well in your marriage, never stop dating!

Do you remember the days when just holding hands would cause your heart to flutter? What happened to those feelings? Now, one partner mutters, "Why should we go out? There's plenty of food in the fridge!"

For some couples, the only conversation they ever exchange concerns the weather and what shows they are going to watch on their separate television sets. There is no excited talk of hopes and plans for the future. Instead, they return home every night from work to what seems more like a cold penitentiary —with a cell mate who doesn't communicate.

Let me encourage you to schedule "date nights" regularly where you share quality time enjoying each other's company, discussing your exciting, bright tomorrow.

THE POWER OF LOVE

Too often we put the cart before the horse—desiring to be married, but not understanding the obligation and responsibility of love.

The moment you say, "I do," you are vowing, "I choose to be involved in your life forever—no matter what your flaws and imperfections may be."

Hopefully, you are willing to look beyond the negative and see the "gold" in your partner.

Love promises, " I am committed to you. I will be loyal and devoted to you forever."

The apostle Paul, writing to the believers at Corinth, shared these words to remember:

- *"Love suffers long..."* (1 Corinthians 14:4). You will never give up on your spouse, regardless of what you may be asked to endure.

- It *"is kind"* (v.4). You will treat your husband or wife as you want to be treated.
- Love *"...does not envy"* (v.4). Even if the wife brings home the largest paycheck, there must be no jealousy in the marriage.
- It *"...does not parade itself, is not puffed up"* (v.4). Love and haughtiness are not compatible.
- It *"...does not behave rudely"* (v.5). Never "show off" or embarrass your spouse in public.
- It *"...does not seek its own"* (v.5). Instead of "me" and "mine," marriage is "we" and "ours."
- Love *"...is not provoked"* (v.5). Foster forgiveness rather than harboring anger.
- Love *"...thinks no evil; does not rejoice in iniquity, but rejoices in the truth"* (vv.5-6). You only see the *good* in your spouse and celebrate what brings glory and honor to God.
- Love *"...bears all things, believes all things, hopes all things, endures all things"* (v.7).

Your divine source of faith and expectation pulls you through every adversity.

- *"Love never fails"* (v.8). Since your love is from God, it is designed to last forever, and the words, "I don't love you anymore," should never be spoken.

THE FORGIVENESS FACTOR

Of all the arrows Satan will aim at your marriage, anger is a favorite in his arsenal.

If you are truly in love and walking with the Lord, why should "losing your cool" be such a constant occurrence? Some couples not only become angry, they remain upset and combative for long periods of time.

As a minister, I find it hard to understand how such people can come to church and praise God, yet they have not spoken to their mate all week!

Even worse, a wife or husband will focus on an event from the past and hold it over their spouse for *life*. This lack of forgiveness will stifle both your marital and spiritual growth.

If the individual who has made an error has asked God for forgiveness, why shouldn't you forgive too?

AGREE QUICKLY

Remember, love *"...keeps no record of wrongs"* (1 Corinthians 13:5 NIV). If you write in a journal or diary, limit the entries to *"...whatever things are noble, whatever things are just, whatever things are pure, whatever things are lovely, whatever things are of good report"* (Philippians 4:8).

Putting this into practice will keep you on the right path.

Jesus tells you to *"Agree with your adversary quickly"* (Matthew 5:25). Instead of allowing faults to fester, snatch them up by the root so they don't ruin your growth and development.

Avoid the temptation to drag up past failures, saying, "I remember what you did last week and hope it doesn't happen again."

Forgive and forget what is in the past—deal with today!

In a sound, solid marriage, the more anniversaries you celebrate the fewer arguments you should have. This becomes a demonstration of your vow "to love and comfort."

7

"Will you honor and keep...?"

*J*ust because Scripture tells us a wife is to obey her husband does not exempt him from treating her with the utmost respect.

In fact, God views spouses as equals— *"heirs together of the grace of life"* (1 Peter 3:7).

In the marriage ceremony, both the bride and groom are asked, "Will you honor and keep...?" This is based on God's Word since husbands are to, "...[give] *honor to the wife, as unto the weaker vessel"* (v.7).

Likewise, the wife is to esteem and respect the man she has chosen to live with for the rest of her days (Ephesians 5:22-24).

Since women are usually physically smaller than their male counterparts, the man is seen as the protector and provider. But don't let the term "weaker vessel" lull you into the belief women are not strong—just ask any mother what stamina it took to endure childbirth!

DEMONSTRATING ESTEEM

Honor is defined as having "high regard" and showing "great respect." Let me share seven specific ways a husband can demonstrate the high value and admiration he holds for his spouse:

1. Recognize and applaud her accomplishments.
2. Assist in developing her talents and abilities.
3. Help her fulfill her dreams and aspirations.
4. Practice common courtesies at home and in public.
5. Speak to her with respect.
6. Always show her dignity and esteem.
7. Treat her like a queen—placing her on a pedestal.

FOUR "HONOR" PRINCIPLES

What happens when the shoe is on the other foot? How are wives supposed to honor their husbands? Consider these four principles:

1. Your "industry" should be his greatest wealth.

The wife is not to sit idly by while her spouse is providing for her needs. She is to be resourceful and industrious.

Economic realities during the past several decades have resulted in millions of women entering the work force rather than being stay-at-home moms. In either case, women contribute significantly to the stability of the family.

As a wife, every hour you spend cleaning the home, washing clothes or taking care of a child brings honor to your husband and to the marriage.

King Solomon, who wrote of the "virtuous

woman," didn't depict her as sitting around twiddling her thumbs. She, *"...rises while it is yet night, and provides food for her household"* (Proverbs 31:15). *"She makes linen garments and sells them, and supplies sashes for the merchants"* (v.24).

When you multiply what is in your hand, you demonstrate honor toward those you love.

2. Your "economy" should be his safest reward.

A friend once told me, "I'm petrified every time my wife goes shopping with our credit card."

Let's hope this is not an issue in your home. Wives, you honor your husband by knowing and practicing sound fiscal management.

One of the greatest virtues a woman can possess is to be thrifty.

I pray it can be said of you: *"The heart of her husband safely trusts her; so he will have no lack of gain"* (Proverbs 31:11).

3. Your lips should always speak faithful counsel.

Some men dread coming home from work because their wives are waiting, armed with a verbal tirade—as if they were spitting razor blades from their mouth!

If you are going to rip him to shreds, I can guarantee he is not listening.

Remember the story of Samson and Delilah? She didn't learn the secret of his strength by blatant demands or brute force. Instead, seductively, *"... she lulled him to sleep on her knees"* (Judges 16:19).

You however, are to be a faithful counselor —encouraging and building strength in the man you love; edifying, not demeaning. The woman of Proverbs 31, *"...opens her mouth with wisdom, and on her tongue is the law of kindness"* (v.26).

4. Your prayers must be his most able advocate in heaven's court.

Make it a passion of life to be an intercessor for your husband—even laying before the Lord daily and waiting to hear from God.

What will be the outcome of your prayerful effort? You will be giving him godly counsel instead of your personal opinion or a reflection of your emotions.

Your mate needs to know what the Lord is saying, not what you heard on "Oprah" or read in a popular magazine.

When you don't know how to pray for your spouse, ask God's Spirit to guide you. Remember, *"...the Spirit Himself makes intercession for us...according to the will of God"* (Romans 8:26-27).

"FOR KEEPS!"

What you honor you want to *keep*—forever and ever!

As you prepare to repeat your marriage vows, you are announcing to your future spouse and before the invited guests, "Out of every other person on the planet, I have chosen to be with you for the rest of my life."

This is not a fishing excursion where if you don't like what you catch you can throw it back in the sea!

Your vow is to honor and "keep!"

Loss of respect—and eventual separation or

divorce—happens because we are prepared for marriage mentally and emotionally, but sadly, not spiritually. Without a personal relationship with Christ, when trouble comes knocking, you have no higher power to call upon.

If marriage to you is only about sex, you are in for a rude awakening! The waters of true intimacy run much deeper.

Without deep-rooted respect for your spouse, you are simply "using" your partner for personal gratification.

Before you take this great leap of faith called marriage, make certain you are prepared to honor your partner for life.

8

"...for better for worse, for richer for poorer..."

$\mathcal{O}$n this memorable occasion, you are making a vow "from this day forward"—

- Not until your spouse gets on your nerves!
- Not until you reach the point where you explode, saying, "I didn't think I was going to marry someone who talked so much!"
- Not until you're tired of a spouse who never agrees with you!

The very words "for better or for worse," tell you in advance that bad times will surely surface.

Life is not always smooth sailing, and since adversity is common to the human experience, one day may be a euphoric "ten," while the next plummets to a "zero."

TAKE A CLOSE LOOK!

In the dating stage of the relationship you may never have the opportunity to discover how the person you are about to marry handles a crisis. This is why I advise young couples not to rush blindly into marriage.

Carefully examine the emotional reactions of your mate in stressful situations. If he or she does not handle adversity well *before* the union, I can guarantee things will not change.

Marrying a person who already carries a truckload of emotional baggage invites a whole new set of circumstances. When the "worse" of "for better or for worse" rears its ugly head, it only intensifies the tendencies which already exist.

In the process of falling in love, it's easy to overlook faults and convince yourself, "I can cause her to change," or "I'm going to make him my 'project.'"

How naive! People rarely change—and the old adage still rings true: "What you see is what you get!" If you firmly believe this is the right decision, *you* are the one who must be willing to change.

MAKE SOME MUSIC

Once you are married, continually remind yourself, "What adjustment do I need to make today so we can live more harmoniously?"

Living together in "concert" means a melody must be played—and when you fail to play the proper notes there is dissonance.

Should there be a root of bitterness hidden in your heart, allow the Holy Spirit to remove it. If not, one day your children will act in rebellion and you'll wonder, "Where did that negative spirit spring from?"

You won't need to search far—it's a branch grown from the stubbornness of your own heart.

The Bible says, *"...let us lay aside every weight, and the sin which so easily ensnares us, and let us run with endurance the race that is set before us"* (Hebrews 12:1).

81

TRIALS ARE GUARANTEED

Let me offer this word of caution. Just because you have chosen to follow Christ doesn't innoculate you permanently from trouble. Jesus says, *"In the world you will have tribulation; but be of good cheer, I have overcome the world"* (John 16:33).

In fact, if you *don't* encounter the trials of life, something must be wrong. The Word declares, *"But know this, that in the last days perilous times will come"* (2 Timothy 3:1). And, *"...all who desire to live godly in Christ Jesus will suffer persecution"* (2 Timothy 3:12).

Thank the Lord, there is hope. The psalmist gives us this assurance: *"Many are the afflictions of the righteous, but the Lord delivers him out of them all"* (Psalm 34:19). *"God is our refuge and strength, a very present help in trouble"* (Psalm 46:1).

BRIDGING THE GULF

It's amazing how two people can come together from entirely different backgrounds and form a bond of unity and agreement.

If you have been raised in totally opposite

environments, don't expect the wide gulf to be bridged overnight. There will be a period of adjustment as you learn to respect the opinions of your spouse on literally hundreds of issues—large and small.

What a boring existence if each views life exactly the same way. There would be no need for conversation or compromise.

Be thankful your spouse throws a pebble in the water from time to time to cause some ripples and waves. If handled properly, it can add some much-needed excitement to your marriage.

Relationships grow and blossom when we have differences of opinion and solve problems, but we must never allow diversity to lead to *adversity.*

YOUR CONTRIBUTION

Decide from the first day of your life together that issues will never be discussed in an argumentative fashion. Let your husband or wife know, "Just because we don't see eye to eye on everything doesn't mean I don't love or care for you."

Since you've signed on "Till death do us part," you have a lifetime to work out your diverse views.

When differences surface, instead of blaming each other, ask yourself, "What will be my contribution to the resolution?" As Scripture tells us, *"A word fitly spoken is like apples of gold in settings of silver"* (Proverbs 25:11).

FOR "POORER"?

Professional marriage counselors tell us that financial issues are the number one cause of conflicts in couples.

If you review the history of Wall Street, you'll see stocks soaring to record-breaking highs, only to be followed by shocking slumps. You will experience this same pattern of peaks and valleys in your marriage.

Yet, you made a pledge "for richer for poorer."

It is easy to deal with the "richer" part, but what happens when the flow of finances slows to a trickle? For example, a spouse may be laid off from a job and there is a crimp in the family budget.

When you have to cut back on spending and are forced to put a halt on your free-spending lifestyle, are you going to bail out on your spouse? I pray not.

It is love and commitment which cements a marriage together, not money—or the lack of it.

NO SECRETS

However, since the Bible says, "...money answers everything" (Ecclesiastes 10:19), let me offer this additional advice.

From the start of your married journey together, have a joint checking account where both of you know every detail of the family accounts—at all times. Jointly sign all financial and legal agreements.

I've heard stories of couples who both worked and neither would tell the other how much money they made—with each one paying specific household expenses and filing separate income tax returns. To me,

85

this is an invitation for disaster and sets up a scenario which makes it far too easy to decide on a separation or divorce.

Also, don't listen to those naysayers who tell you, "Keep a secret nest egg in case things go wrong." If you think in those terms, you are *attracting* adversity.

Marriage is a union; you are to share all things in common, including your finances. There should be no situation where you say "This is mine, " and "That is yours." It signals a lack of trust.

"TWO ARE BETTER THAN ONE"

In your vows, you are committing to your partner for life, "I am giving you my word no matter what situation arises, you will not have to face it alone."

God's Word declares, *"Two are better than one, because they have a good reward for their labor. For if they fall, one will lift up his companion. But woe to him who is alone when he falls, for he has no one to help him up. Again, if two lie down together, they will keep warm; but how can one be warm alone?"* (Ecclesiastes 4:9-11).

Yes, there is strength in the union of marriage.

Then Scripture adds, *"And a threefold cord is not quickly broken"* (v. 12).

The three strands are (1) you, (2) your spouse and (3) the Holy Spirit. If you walk in step with the Spirit you have a Teacher and Guide when facing the storms which inevitably will arise.

A TEAM EFFORT

In the game of football, the reason there are "hash marks" chalked on the field is because you have to grind out a victory yard by yard, inch by inch. And if you fail to make progress on the first attempt, you try and try again.

This determination is exactly what is required in marriage. "For better for worse, for richer for poorer," it is a team effort and you must keep moving forward.

Staying true to your vows will lead to a lifetime of happiness and fulfillment.

9

"...in sickness and in health..."

The person who believes he will make it through his days on this earth with zero "sick days," is living in a fool's paradise.

It's an idyllic thought, but because of what took place in the Garden of Eden, we are all born in sin and live in a fallen world. As a result, everyone eventually faces pain, hurt and other physical difficulties.

You, as husband and wife, have made a vow to love each other "in sickness and in health," yet when an illness surfaces we are rarely prepared. It's as if our whole world suddenly crumbles around us.

How you will handle health problems should be discussed at the *start* of your marriage, not when an ambulance rushes you to an emergency room!

Instead of viewing sickness as a scourge which drives you apart, it should be seen as part of God's plan to draw you closer together.

A HOME OF HEALING

Never be ashamed to openly pray for your spouse who is in need of healing. As a believer you should tenderly lay your hands on the person you love, *"And the prayer of faith will save the sick, and the Lord will raise him up"* (James 5:15).

Always look to the source of healing—Christ Himself.

It is through His wounds on the cross you can claim your health.

As it was prophesied, *"He was wounded for our transgressions, He was bruised for our iniquities; the chastisement for our peace was upon Him, and by His stripes we are healed"* (Isaiah 53:5).

Peter echoed these words when he declared Jesus *" bore our sins in His own body on the tree, that we, having died to sins, might live for righteousness—by whose stripes you were healed"* (1 Peter 2:24).

When you fully embrace Jesus' broken body, your own is being restored.

STRENGTH IN WEAKNESS

As a minister I've met many couples whose marriages have actually been strengthened, even love rekindled, through an illness in either the husband or wife. This is why we should thank the Lord for every situation He allows us to go through.

If you read the story of the apostle Paul, he had a *"thorn in the flesh"* which he thought came from Satan (2 Corinthians 12:7).

Of course, Paul wanted this aggravation removed. *"Concerning this thing I pleaded with the Lord three times that it might depart from me"* (v.8). But the Lord replied, *"My grace is sufficient for you, for My strength is made perfect in weakness"* (v.9).

Paul was eventually able to declare to the world, *"For when I am weak, then I am strong"* (v.10).

ROCK SOLID LOVE?

Sir, answer honestly: how will you respond when

your wife falls ill? What if she can't function at the level you expect? Oh, you can handle a cold or the flu for a few days, but how do you react when the situation grows serious, even life threatening —when there are no more physical, intimate relations?

Will the love you pledged at the marriage altar remain rock solid?

Will you be there for her—making sure she doesn't need to worry over the finances or daily chores? Are you sensitive to her needs?

Let's remind ourselves, when we are sick, our spiritual Husband, the Lord, desires for us to be restored to full health. So if you, the husband, are the reflection of the Heavenly Father, you will do everything in your power to make certain your wife is on the road to recovery.

WILL YOU SACRIFICE?

This same counsel applies to the wife. If your husband develops colon or prostate cancer, are you willing to put your personal schedule aside to take care of him? If he is on disability, will you fill in the gap—regardless of the sacrifice involved?

It is a well known fact most men don't handle infirmity well. Let's face it; the majority are big babies when it comes to physical pain.

Also, neither party should ever exaggerate a physical problem as a ploy to test the love of their spouse—or to escape from family obligations.

You are in this marriage together. There will be times of sickness and there will be days of health, but most important, let there be love.

Many people at the outset of marriage never think there will be dark days. Of course, no one plans to be ill, but as I have stated, sickness will come. This is the time when your spouse needs you the most. Withdrawals will be made from the "love bank" like never before.

Don't allow your spouse's account to be overdrawn in your mind; constantly make deposits for them since they are not able to do it for themselves.

10

"Will you forsake all others as long as you both shall live?"

$\mathcal{F}$or many, marriage has become an arrangement of convenience rather than a committed lifetime partnership. Some tie the knot only to satisfy their physical, emotional or financial needs, never taking the time to look at the far-reaching implications of separation or divorce.

When the honeymoon is over and perhaps things are not going as well as you expected, don't make the fatal mistake of allowing either your eyes or your emotions to stray. "Johnny" should not start looking better than your husband. Or, "Jane" more enticing than your wife.

This is especially true of the first year of marriage, which is a tremendous time of adjustment. Both parties go from a life of independence to a life of interdependence, and also seeing the idiosyncracies of their mate on a daily basis.

RECOGNIZE THE WARNINGS

Never reach the point where you find yourself treating others better than you treat your spouse—at work, among friends, or even in church. At the first indication of trouble in your relationship, recognize the warning signs and ask the Lord to renew the love you once had.

Your pledge of fidelity must be mutual. You are promising to lavish love on one another and be faithful "till death do us part"— not until you get mad or grow tired of living together.

Marriage is not a 50-50 proposition as many believe; it requires 100 percent from both parties!

"NO MATTER WHAT"

God says, *"...and they shall become one flesh"* (Genesis 2:24). In today's language this means you are joined together —stuck like glue.

My wife, Deborah, and I, made a covenant that "no matter what," we are together for the long haul! And I can testify to the fact we love one another more at this moment than the day we were married.

Our love is demonstrated and cemented by the small things we do for each other. For example, in the normal course of our daily schedule, I regularly call her and let her know where I am—and she does the same for me. It's a simple thing, but the peace of mind and comfort it gives is priceless.

One Heart, One Rhythm

The relationship between the husband and wife is so sacred it should become two souls with one single thought. The Word tells us, *"...be of one mind...and the God of love and peace will be with you"* (2 Corinthians 13:11).

The soul is the seat of our emotions, desire, affections and will.

Because this is true, we must *will* ourselves to think together with our mate—not separately. As Jesus declares, *"...if two of you agree on earth concerning anything that they ask, it will be done for them by My Father in heaven"* (Matthew 18:19).

For a couple to become "one flesh" requires more than the physical act of sex. There must be one heart, one rhythm and cadence in the relationship. So much so, when people see you together, they think of you as *one!*

You still have your own personality, but there should be no competition in the marriage. Your two lives are forever blended.

A COMMON OBJECTIVE

Scripture asks, *"Can two walk together, unless they are agreed?"* (Amos 3:3).

Because of the Holy Spirit, you are able to bury your own nature and infuse it with that of your spouse. Together you are making one destiny for the marriage itself.

Certainly we have individual callings, but through a God-centered marriage, the two purposes are united for one common objective.

Ask yourself, "What does the Lord want to accomplish through both of us that we could not do alone?"

The person you are going to marry should automatically compliment the goals and aspirations you already possess.

As Scripture tells us, the woman is made for the man (1 Corinthians 11:8). She is a helper and her gifts and talents are to assist her husband.

YOUR TRUE PARTNER

What obligation does the groom have? When a man proposes, asking the woman of his dreams to become his wife, she must become a viable partner—the vice president of your corporation. This means she has vital input into what is going on.

Your wife is not a person who just comes along side you every once and awhile to offer help—or to be held at arm's length. No, she is a true life partner.

The problem in many marriages is that one spouse wants the other to be performance oriented, silently saying, "I will love you —as long as you do things my way!"

Such a lopsided union is not based on mutual respect.

The woman you are marrying is a daughter of the Lord. She has been entrusted into your care and you have a divine obligation to forsake all other women and to love and provide just for her.

"WHAT ANNIVERSARY?

Generally, women are nostalgic, romantic creatures by nature who likely remember every detail of their first date—what they wore and where they went. She can probably even recall what appetizer and entrée were ordered from the menu!

As newlyweds, don't be surprised to arrive home one day and hear your wife exclaim, "This is our anniversary."

"What anniversary?" you nervously respond.

"The very first time we went out together!" she says. It's important to her.

Spread Your Wings

Will you be observant enough to know when the woman you love is unhappy or struggling? At these times will you speak hope and life to her—instead of heating the coals with criticism and judgment?

Be like Ezekiel, who declared, *"And when I passed by you and saw you struggling in your own blood* [in your life], *I said to your blood, "Live!"* (Ezekiel 16:6).

I hope you will be able to say, *"I made you thrive like a plant in the field; and you grew, matured, and became very beautiful"* (v.7).

You have a duty to cherish, nurture and protect your wife.

In the words of Scripture, *"When I...looked upon you, indeed your time was the time of love; so I spread My wing over you..."* (vv.8-9). *"I clothed you with fine linen and covered you with silk. I adorned you with ornaments, put bracelets on your wrists, and a chain on your neck"* (vv.10-11).

A CALL TO RECONCILIATION

Many hurt individuals want to know what recourse they have when their unbelieving spouse walks out on them. Instead of giving you my opinion, here is what God states through the apostle Paul: *"Now to the married I command, yet not I but the Lord: A wife is not to depart from her husband"* (1 Corinthians 7:10).

The Bible teaches that even if a woman *does* leave, she is to either, *"...remain unmarried or be reconciled to her husband. And a husband is not to divorce his wife"* (v.11).

God has called us to a life of reconciliation and peace. Jesus proclaimed, *"Blessed are the peacemakers, for they shall be called sons of God"* (Matthew 5:9).

Regardless of temptation, we must keep our flesh under subjection because it is written, *"...be sure your sin will find you out"* (Numbers 32:23).

HE IS CALLING YOU BACK

When discontentment creeps into your marriage, step back and view the problem from God's perspective. Mentally, retrace your steps to the wedding altar and hear yourself repeating your vows.

Realize you are united with both the Lord and your spouse. With this knowledge, if you try to walk away you will hear His voice tenderly calling, *"Return, O backsliding children,' says the Lord; 'for I am married to you'"* (Jeremiah 3:14).

God has you safe and secure in the palm of His hand—and no one can pluck you out (John 10:28).

Since these are the Lord's rules for marriage, why should you, His child, attempt to destroy what He has joined together?

On your wedding day you are making a vow to forsake all others—as long as you both shall live!

It is utterly important for a spouse to share with their mate any inner struggles concerning their relationship. This accomplishes two things:

1. Your mate knows now how to pray for you and keep you spiritually covered.
2. The honesty and truth factor is maintained by being able to be transparent with one another.

Be assured that truth strengthens relationships and prevents hidden secrets from becoming open wounds!

11

"I pledge to you my faith."

One of the most overlooked phrases in the marriage vows is the following: "I pledge to you my faith."

In essence you are saying, "I am making a promise to always be faithful to you."

The "virtuous wife" described in Proverbs possessed a value which was "far above rubies." Why? Because, *The heart of her husband safely trusts her*" (Proverbs 31:11).

WHAT HAPPENED TO BELIEF?

Having total faith and trust in your spouse stretches far beyond fidelity. It means you believe so deeply in the one you love that his or her imperfections, faults and shortcomings are totally and permanently dismissed from your thoughts.

Unfortunately, many marriages are plagued with conflict and strife because small mistakes become magnified and minor errors mushroom into major barriers. Instead of focusing on the issue at hand, we often paint the problem with a broad brush—"You *always* act like this!"

What happened to belief? Where is the trust? What about the undying faith you have pledged?

The Bible tells us we must not create a scorecard of offenses because love, *"... keeps no record of wrongs"* (1 Corinthians 13:5 NIV).

Pay close attention to the words of Jesus regarding how unforgiveness affects our ability to commune with God. The Lord says, *"...if you have anything against anyone* [including your spouse], *forgive him, that your Father in heaven may also forgive you your trespasses. But if you do not forgive, neither will your Father in heaven forgive your trespasses"* (Mark 11:25-26).

FAITH INVOLVES FORGIVENESS

Sadly, you demonstrate your loss of faith the moment you stomp your foot and announce, "I'm sick and tired of you and I can't take it anymore!"

But what happens when you go to God in prayer regarding other matters in your life? According to the Scripture you have just read, the Lord turns a deaf ear when you hold an unforgiving spirit toward your mate.

This is why we are counseled, *"do not let the sun go down on your wrath"* (Ephesians 4:26).

In marriage, faith involves forgiveness— regardless of who is right or wrong.

Peter asked Jesus, "How many times should I forgive? Seven times?"

Jesus answered, *"I do not say to you, up to seven times, but up to seventy times seven"* (Matthew 18:22)—that's 490 acts of forgiveness!

A SIGN OF MATURITY

It must break the heart of God when He sees two people living under the same roof, eating at the same table, sleeping in the same bed and riding in the same car, yet they harbor a faithless, unforgiving spirit. How can this be called a true marriage?

Don't run the risk of tampering with God's plan for a union based on faith, hope and love.

Whether you have been married one month, one year or are celebrating your silver anniversary, the Lord expects you to live by your vows and demonstrate His divine principles every day.

Complete faith in your spouse is a sign of spiritual maturity.

A PERMANENT COVENANT

There is a powerful correlation between the trust

we place in Christ and the faith we have in our husband or wife. In both instances, *"...we walk by faith, not by sight"* (2 Corinthians 5:7).

Here is the promise God makes to His children: *"My lovingkindness I will not utterly take...nor allow My faithfulness to fail. My covenant I will not break, nor alter the word that has gone out of My lips"* (Psalm 89:33-34).

I pray you have made an eternal vow to the partner the Lord has graciously given you by honoring the words: "I pledge to you my faith."

12

"With this ring, I thee wed."

*D*uring the wedding vows, the minister will ask the couple to join their right hands. This has symbolic meaning, since Christ is in heaven, seated at the right hand of God (Hebrews 10:12). It also signifies the covenant and agreement you are making with each other.

Finally, the question is asked of the groom, "What token do you give as a symbol of your affection, sincerity and fidelity?"

The husband-to-be takes the wedding ring and places it on the third finger of his bride's left hand. This practice stems from an ancient tradition because it was believed the vein from the "ring finger" was connected directly to the heart.

Next, the woman is asked the same question, and likewise, she presents a ring as a token of her love.

AN UNENDING CIRCLE

Even though a wedding band is small in size, it is extremely large in significance. Being made of a precious metal such as gold, platinum or silver, it serves as a constant reminder that our love has great value—it is not "tawdry" or "common."

The formation of the ring—made in a circle—tells us true love is unending and is designed by God to be continuous.

The empty space in the center of the ring is what I call "the infinity of uncertainty," because you do not know what tomorrow will hold. In reality, however, the ring depicts the cycle of life—as we journey from heartache to joy, from failure to success, from being alone to falling in love.

SEALING YOUR MARRIAGE

In the ceremony, the words, "With this ring, I thee wed," verbalize the covenant, but when you place the ring on the finger of your partner, the vow is sealed. In earlier centuries, it was *only* when the rings were exchanged that the marriage became legal and binding.

Throughout history, rings have not only been a symbol of love, they also speak of authority. Kings and religious leaders have worn a "signet"—or ring—to stamp their seal of approval on important documents.

"WHAT'S MINE IS YOURS"

The pledge, "With all my worldly goods I thee endow" becomes meaningful when these tokens are exchanged. However, do the bride and groom really know what they are declaring?

In this context, to "endow" means to provide income or financial support. With the ring, you are declaring "What's mine is yours. Everything we have is common property."

When a couple brings all their earthly possessions to the marriage, they do so in complete faith.

However, I have counseled wives who were told by their mothers, "You better keep a little nest-egg on the side for a rainy day, just in case things don't go well."

With such advice, the mother is encouraging her daughter to be deceitful. Thus, when the bride declares, "With all my worldly goods," it is a lie. This is why we must be totally honest when we announce we are giving all to our partner for life.

Additionally, a man often deceitfully refuses to disclose how much he earns on his job or in his business. There are also some men who hide their money when they come home, which is just as out of order as the wife who conceals what she has.

"WHAT IS YOUR REQUEST?"

A wedding ring is much more than a piece of beautiful jewelry. It is a visible symbol of trust.

Before the marriage, the groom promises his bride everything imaginable—and he would include the sun, moon and stars if he could!

Such devotion parallels what took place in Queen Esther's day. When she entered the royal court and touched the top of the golden scepter, the king asked the woman he loved, *"What do you wish, Queen Esther? What is your request? It shall be given to you—up to half the kingdom!"* (Esther 5:3).

Thankfully, when the king was put to the test, he stood by his vow—even though it resulted in the banishment of his own prime minister. Because the king honored his word, Esther's people escaped annihilation and were given a preferred status in the land. The decree was sealed, *"...with the king's signet ring"* (Esther 8:10).

A REMINDER OF YOUR COVENANT

During the tough times of marriage there may be moments you wish you could pull the ring from your finger and spin it away. Yet the very sight of this band of gold or silver brings you back to the moment when you made a covenant in the name of the Father, the Son and the Holy Spirit. It reminds you of the vow you confessed before God and man on your wedding day.

Your promise of eternal love is what makes the ring you wear more valuable than any price which was paid for its purchase.

Remember, marriage should be a knitting of two hearts and not just the exchange of rings.

13

"Till death do us part."

When my wife and I were first married, life wasn't exactly a bed of roses. I can still remember driving our old Chevrolet—and hanging onto the door handles to keep them from flying open!

When the rats and mice scurried around our little house, she could have complained, "What have I got myself into?" But she didn't—not even when our house burned down.

You see, we made the decision our vows were for keeps, regardless of the circumstances.

Even *before* we were married, there was an unbreakable bond. For example, one evening we had an argument just before I headed for the church I pastored. However, when I arrived, I was upset and told the elders, "I have to leave. I can't preach tonight!"

Immediately, I rushed back and knocked on her door again and again until she finally opened it. Then I told her, "I'm not leaving here until we make things right. How can I stand before my congregation when there are problems between us?"

We solved our differences and I drove back to the church where I was able to minister with a clean heart.

NAVIGATING THROUGH THE STORM

Conflicts are inevitable, but they should not lead to divorce unless there is infidelity or abuse. Remember, God *hates* divorce (Malachi 2:16).

Storms will arise in every marriage, and when they do, turn to the Master of the Seas. When the disciples were about to drown because of the crashing waves, they *"cried out"* (Matthew 14:26), and Jesus came walking on the water.

When you are in the midst of turmoil, removing your wedding band in anger won't solve the problem. You're still married and, with God's help, you can navigate your way through life's tempest together.

DEFEND YOUR MARRIAGE!

The moment a husband or wife decides not to fight for their marriage, adversity intensifies.

Be like Nehemiah, who was under attack as he rebuilt the walls of Jerusalem. He told the people, *"...fight for your brethren, your sons, your daughters, your wives, and your houses"* (Nehemiah 4:14).

Just because you come to the realization your spouse isn't perfect—and you're not so hot yourself— don't despair and throw in the towel!

The Bible tells us we are *all* imperfect. As the apostle Paul confessed, *"For I know that in me (that is, in my flesh) nothing good dwells"* (Romans 7:18).

DON'T LOOK BACK

One couple, who had been together for many years, told me, "There was a time when we seriously considered ending our marriage, but we finally realized the vows we made to each other were far more important than the temporary crisis we were passing through."

The Bible warns, *"Do not let your mouth cause your flesh to sin, nor say before the messenger of God that it was an error. Why should God be angry at your excuse and destroy the work of your hands?"* (Ecclesiastes 5:6).

Since the Lord takes no pleasure in our failure, don't enter into a commitment you do not intend to keep. Never forget, in matrimony, you are representing Almighty God—the epitome of truth. Here's what the Lord says concerning finishing what you start:

- *"Now the just shall live by faith; But if anyone draws back, My soul has no pleasure in him"* (Hebrews 10:38).
- *"No one, having put his hand to the plow, and looking back, is fit for the kingdom of God."* (Luke 9:62).
- *"For which of you, intending to build a tower, does not sit down first and count the cost, whether he has enough to finish it"* (Luke 14:28).

Your Heavenly Father desires for you to *"...bear much fruit"* (John 15:8), so how can you glorify Him if you walk out on what He has ordained?

Before commitment there must be conviction—a convincing spirit within you that no matter what transpires you will not abandon your vows.

Your trust must be in God, not in yourself. The Almighty says, *"Cursed is the man who trusts in man and makes flesh his strength"* (Jeremiah 17:5).

It's not our human ability, but His almighty power!

DIVORCE IS NOT AN OPTION

The minister announces, "What God has joined together let no man put asunder."

In the heat of anger, don't be drawn to or swayed by a divorce lawyer who is only too willing to take your money if you'll sign on the dotted line. And if you ever hear the words, "no-fault divorce," don't believe it! Of course, someone is at fault!

Why should you pull apart what God has joined together? The man or woman who looks to divorce as a solution is not just forsaking the marriage, they are essentially giving up on life.

Your love should create a bond so strong, absolutely nothing can tear it apart. This is why you should never take advice from people who have been divorced and are still bitter—since misery loves company!

Erase from your mind that separation or divorce is an option. It's not!

Since God has brought you into a physical and spiritual union, He will make a way for your marriage to succeed.

If Satan attacks your family, tell him, "Get out of my house! You can't have my children or my marriage!"

The Bible encourages us with these words: *"... in*

due season we shall reap, if we faint not" (Galatians 6:9 KJV).

"SHE DESPISED HIM"

A young woman named Michal, the daughter of King Saul, admired David and won his heart. However, it took time for him to see her dark side.

When David entered the city after recovering the Ark of the Covenant, Michal, *"...watched from a window. And when she saw King David leaping and dancing before the Lord, she despised him in her heart"* (2 Samuel 16).

Think of it! The man she was so deeply in love with, she now hated—all because he seemed out of character.

When David returned to bless his household, Michal mocked him. Instead of greeting him saying, "How wonderful to see you," she couldn't get past the fact David had taken off his royal robes in public and was seen only wearing his priestly garment. She chided, *"How the king of Israel has distinguished himself today, disrobing in the sight of the slave girls of his servants as any vulgar fellow would!"* (v.20).

123

She descended from royalty and was distraught that he was not appropriately dressed as a king.

DON'T JUMP TO CONCLUSIONS

This is a lesson for every relationship. If you allow your thoughts to linger and fester, you run the risk of releasing feelings which will be detrimental to your marriage.

Michal was upset because other women were looking at her man—even though he was fully clothed in his priestly garment.

David, indignant, went on the defensive, telling his wife the dancing, *"...was before the Lord, who chose me rather than your father or anyone from his house when he appointed me ruler over the Lord's people Israel—I will celebrate before the Lord"* (v.21).

If you read the story, David continued even further, telling her, "If you didn't like that, just wait. The next time I will be even more undignified! (v. 22).

Michal was punished by God for her actions, and she *"...had no children to the day of her death"* (v.23).

The Lord expects us to love, cherish and nurture the most important relationship of life. How much better it would have been if Michal had been the woman written about by King Solomon: *"She opens her mouth with wisdom, and on her tongue is the law of kindness"* (Proverbs 31:26).

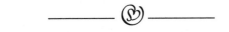

We can all be guilty of inciting a riot in our relationship by the tone and emotion of our words.

Take the time to understand the reason and motivation behind the actions of your mate—and avoid accusing unjustly. Otherwise, you may expose your own immaturity and insecurity.

EXAMINE YOUR HEART

From the moment of marriage, God expects your eyes, mind and emotions to be reserved for only your spouse. This is why Jesus, when speaking of one of the Ten Commandments, "You shall not commit adultery, added, *"But I say to you that whoever looks at a woman to lust for her has already committed adultery with her in his heart"* (Matthew 5:28).

125

HOW LONG IS FOREVER?

One frustrated wife told me, "We've been married for two years and he still hasn't changed!"

I reminded her she didn't marry for "change," but for "love." The only time limit God sets for your marriage is "Till death."

Regardless of the trials and setbacks, let your commitment remain steadfast and pull you through. As the Bible states, *"Love suffers long and is kind"* (1 Corinthians 13:4).

Forever is just what it says—*forever!* There is no clause in God's Word which reads, "If you don't feel like going on, you can end the marriage at your convenience."

BY HIS SPIRIT!

The only reason we can honestly say, "Till death do us part" is because we walk by faith, not by sight. This commitment is possible because we have chosen to, *"...be strong in the Lord and in the power of His might"* (Ephesians 6:10).

A permanent, loving marriage is not the result of

your human efforts, rather because of what God has placed within you: "'*Not by might nor by power, but by My Spirit,' Says the Lord of hosts*" (Zechariah 4:6).

When the Holy Spirit resides within, you will have the power to overcome every obstacle—even putting up with behavior in your mate perhaps you don't understand!

GOD'S HAMMER AND CHISEL

The two of you stood before the altar in your tuxedo and wedding gown, looked at each other and thought "This is forever!"

If this is true, why do you want to climb out of the boat at the first clap of thunder?

God's grace is sufficient for every situation. Paul declared, "*we...glory in tribulations, knowing that tribulation produces perseverance; and perseverance, character; and character, hope*" (Romans 6:3-4).

There is a place for trials and tests. Perhaps God is using a hammer and chisel to prepare you both for greater service in His Kingdom.

Even when you see dark clouds forming, the sun is behind them, waiting to break through.

127

14

"I now pronounce you husband and wife."

*F*inally, the ceremony has neared its conclusion and the bride and groom hear these life-changing words: "And so, by the power vested in me by this state and by Almighty God, I now pronounce you man and wife. In the name of the Father, and of the Son and of the Holy Ghost. Amen."

While it may mark the end of the long-awaited wedding, it signals the beginning of the most exciting adventure you will ever experience.

A "KINGDOM CONSCIOUSNESS"

From this moment forward, you are not just a statistic, a husband or wife, but a person who is to reflect the life of Christ.

God intends for marriage to be a stabilizing force in the world. He is saying, "I have united you together to accomplish my purpose."

This is why He desires to place a "Kingdom consciousness" deep inside both of you—which will cause you to constantly gravitate toward Him, and each other.

If our marriages are not built on a strong foundation, the church itself will be at risk. After all, the church is just a structure of wood, brick or stone, but with the Lord's help, we are the ones who cement it together and give it life.

If your union is not rock solid, you cause
God's house to become unstable.

Because of your covenant relationship, *"as living stones,* [you] *are being built up a spiritual house, a holy priesthood, to offer up spiritual sacrifices acceptable to God through Jesus Christ"* (1 Peter 2:5)

You are the bricks which He desires to shape so

they will fit perfectly into His sanctuary. However, if you will not allow yourself to be submitted to the Lord, how can He use you in His divine plan?

When Solomon built the great temple, the Bible records that he worked on the stones before they were ever brought to the construction site (1 Kings 6:7). As a result, not a hammer or a chisel was needed—each stone was a perfect fit.

This is because metal represented war and Solomon had peace during his reign. Therefore, we should desire to anchor our marriage in peace.

Are you ready and willing to allow the Lord to prepare you for His service?

DEMONSTRATE THE ATTRIBUTES OF GOD

Because we are created in the likeness of God, our behavior is to be a reflection of His image and consistent with His character.

Our Heavenly Father is the totality of every quality mentioned in Scripture. He didn't just *form* these attributes, He *embodies* them.

God is constant—and He is always what He

131

declares. He is the same, *"...yesterday, today, and forever" (Hebrews 13:8)*. As James writes, *"Every good gift and every perfect gift is from above, and comes down from the Father of lights, with whom there is no variation or shadow of turning"* (James 1:17).

From the moment we accept Christ as our personal Savior, the Holy Spirit begins to change us. As the apostle Paul explains, *"...when one turns to the Lord, the veil is taken away. Now the Lord is the Spirit; and where the Spirit of the Lord is, there is liberty. But we all, with unveiled face, beholding as in a mirror the glory of the Lord, are being transformed into the same image from glory to glory, just as by the Spirit of the Lord"* (2 Corinthians 3:16-18).

Now, as husband and wife, you have an obligation to daily manifest these seven attributes of God:

1. BE MERCIFUL AND GRACIOUS

There will be occasions when you think your spouse doesn't deserve your mercy, yet you demonstrate it because it is a virtue of your Heavenly Father.

Scripture tells us, *"The Lord is merciful and*

gracious, slow to anger, and abounding in mercy" (Psalm 103:8).

Don't respond in haste or out of emotion, giving way to your feelings in the heat of battle.

Learn to pause and let God's Spirit of grace guide your words and actions.

2. BE COMPASSIONATE

During the earthly ministry of Jesus, He attracted large crowds and touched many lives because, *"He was moved with compassion for them"* (Matthew 9:36).

As a believer, this same virtue must be evident in the way you treat your spouse. In the words of Paul, *"...as God's chosen people...clothe yourselves with compassion"* (Colossians 3:12 NIV).

3. BE TENDER AND GENTLE

Some people read the Bible and only see a God filled with vengeance and wrath. However, if you look closer, you will find His anger is directed toward those who have chosen to disobey His commands.

To the believer, God rules with a gentle hand and a tender heart. In fact, "gentleness" is included in the fruit of the Spirit (Galatians 5:22-23).

I pray from the moment you utter the words, "I do," you will follow the advice of Jesus when He says, *"Take My yoke upon you and learn from Me, for I am gentle and lowly in heart, and you will find rest for your souls"* (Matthew 11:29).

It's important to know the *"...beauty of a gentle and quiet spirit...is very precious in the sight of God"* (1 Peter 3:4).

4. BE PATIENT

If you want your romance to last through the years, relax! Since God doesn't make two people alike, your pace and schedule will inevitably vary from that of your partner.

Ask the Lord to give you a double dose of His prescription for patience!

When David was consumed with fear and anxiety, he said, *"I waited patiently for the Lord; and He inclined to me, and heard my cry"* (Psalm 40:1).

Since God is longsuffering, you can claim this quality too. *"Now may the God of patience and comfort grant you to be like-minded toward one another"* (Romans 5:15).

5. BE FAITHFUL

The key to remaining true to your husband or wife is to understand that God expects us to emulate His eternal attribute—faithfulness.

The Lord is the ultimate promise keeper. *"Indeed I have spoken it; I will also bring it to pass. I have purposed it; I will also do it"* (Isaiah 46:11).

These words must also reflect how you view your vows—you have declared them publicly, now is the time to *live* them.

6. BE LOVING

Just as God "so loved" us, a man is to *"...so love his wife even as himself; and the wife see that she reverence her husband"* Ephesians 5:33 KJV).

GILBERT COLEMAN, JR.

As we find in the life of Christ, the commitment we make should be one of service and sacrifice—a true demonstration of unconditional love.

When the Lord is at the heart of your marriage, *"...your faith grows exceedingly, and the love of every one of you abounds toward each other"* (2 Thessalonians 1:3).

7. BE FORGIVING

Continuing to harbor resentment will not only create a dark cloud over your relationship, it constructs a barrier between you and God. This is why we are counseled, *"...if you have anything against anyone, forgive him, that your Father in heaven may also forgive you your trespasses"* (Mark 11:25).

Forgiveness requires a short memory, because when we lose our ability to forget, we become extremely selfish. It's unfortunate if a husband or wife continually brings up past mistakes as a way of manipulating the relationship—making the spouse pay for an error again and again—this is witchcraft!

It is well worth repeating that love, *"...keeps no record of wrongs:"* (1 Corinthians 13:5).

BE SENSITIVE TO THE SPIRIT

A passionate love for your partner is admirable, but it should never become so dominant that you grow immune to God's voice.

It is through His Holy Spirit you will find the guidance and direction you so desperately need.

After many years of ministry and counseling, I've witnessed the disasters caused when either the husband or wife depends on personal feelings or the "flesh" to make decisions. It is a heartache waiting to happen!

As you begin your life together, pay close attention to these words: *"...if you live according to the flesh you will die; but if by the Spirit you put to death the deeds of the body, you will live"* (Romans 8:13).

The reason so many are unable to handle marriage is because they don't understand what it means to be dead to selfish desires and resurrected unto Christ.

A MARRIAGE MADE IN HEAVEN

Together, strive to stay in constant fellowship and

communion with the Lord. Glorious indeed is our future when we are lifted higher by His miracle-working power and begin to see our lives from His vantage point.

Today, tomorrow and until you stand before the King of kings, may your marriage be a ministry which testifies to the amazing grace of God.

I pray the principles we have discussed will result in the loving relationship the Lord envisions for you. As we have learned on these pages:

- Make certain you are united spiritually before you are joined physically.
- Before saying your vows, pause for a moment and contemplate the moral principles you are being *commanded* to keep.
- It is imperative that your sins have been washed in the precious blood of Calvary before you enter "holy matrimony."
- See your vows as a sacred and eternal covenant.
- Forgive and forget what is in the past—deal with today!

- Be prepared to honor your partner for life.
- Make certain, "For better for worse, for richer for poorer," it is a team effort.
- Whether in sickness or health, thank the Lord for every situation He allows us to experience.
- Vow to "forsake all others as long as you both shall live."
- Pledge your undying faith and trust.
- Proudly wear your wedding ring as a symbol of your eternal love.
- Declare before God that you will never abandon your vows.
- Daily demonstrate the attributes of God.

Having made these commitments, you can honestly look into the eyes of the partner the Lord has given you and express with a heart filled with love, "TILL DEATH DO US PART."

NOTES

_____

_____

_____

_____

_____

_____

_____

_____

_____

_____

_____

_____

_____

_____

_____

FOR A COMPLETE LIST OF BOOKS
AND OTHER RESOURCES, OR TO SCHEDULE
THE AUTHOR FOR SPEAKING ENGAGEMENTS,
CONTACT:

BISHOP GILBERT COLEMAN, JR.
FREEDOM CHRISTIAN BIBLE FELLOWSHIP
6100 WEST COLUMBIA AVENUE
PHILADELPHIA, PA 19151

PHONE: 215-477-0800
FAX: 215-473-1640
TOLL FREE: 800-822-6335
EMAIL: FCBFChurch@aol.com
INTERNET: www.freedomworldwide.net